12 WOMEN IN SCIENCE AND TECHNOLOGY

by Brianna L. DeVore

12 STORY LIBRARY
MORE TO EXPLORE

www.12StoryLibrary.com

12-Story Library is an imprint of Bookstaves.

Photographs ©: NASA, cover, 1; PD, 4; Harris & Ewing/Library of Congress, 5; PD, 5; CaymanTourism/YouTube, 6; Kayleen N./YouTube, 6; Lotus_studio/Shutterstock.com, 7; thegameawards/YouTube, 8; Howard Shaw/CC4.0, 9; Activision/PD, 9; NASA, 10; NASA, 11; Fred MACARRY/CC2.0, 12; Franck Cabrol/CC3.0, 13; Shokc/CC4.0, 14; Tesseract2/CC3.0, 15; PD, 15; Aubrey Gemignani/NASA, 16; NASA/Johns Hopkins Applied Physics Laboratory/ Southwest Research Institute, National Optical Astronomy Observatory, 17; WORLD TV HINDI/ YouTube, 17; Jim Bennett/Getty Images, 18; Trueffelpix/Shutterstock.com, 19; NASA, 19; PD, 20; Designua/Shutterstock.com, 21; SITNBoston/CC4.0, 21; Yoshiaki Kita/TEDxKyoto/ CC2.0, 22; Stephen McCarthy/Collision via Sportsfile/CC2.0, 23; PD, 24; monicaodo/ Shutterstock.com, 25; Sikarin Thanachaiary/World Economic Forum/CC2.0, 26; Bloomberg/ YouTube, 27; PD, 28; Washington Area Spark/CC2.0, 29

ISBN
9781632357823 (hardcover)
9781632358912 (paperback)
9781645820628 (ebook)

Library of Congress Control Number: 2019938617

Printed in the United States of America
September 2019

About the Cover
Annie Easley.

Access free, up-to-date content on this topic plus a full digital version of this book. Scan the QR code on page 31 or use your school's login at 12StoryLibrary.com.

Table of Contents

1 Beatrice Medicine: Studying Native American Cultures

Beatrice Medicine was born in 1923 on the Standing Rock Reservation in South Dakota. She was a member of the Sihasapa Lakota Sioux tribe. Her Lakota name was Hinsha Waste Agli Win. It means "Returns Victorious with a Red Horse Woman." This is a powerful name among Native Americans. Medicine's aunt, Ella Cara Deloria, was one of the first indigenous women to work as an anthropologist.

In 1945, Medicine received her bachelor's degree from South Dakota State University. She went on to earn master's degrees in anthropology and sociology. In 1983, she received her PhD in anthropology.

Medicine studied Native Americans throughout the United States. She stayed with different tribes and learned how they lived. She shared her findings with the tribes. She helped them in whatever ways she could, from translating to assisting in court cases.

In the early 1900s, anthropologists harmed indigenous people or treated them unfairly. Many Native Americans learned not to trust them. Through her work, Medicine began to heal those wounds. She died in December 2005 at 82 years old.

An anthropologist conducts a recording session with Blackfoot Mountain Chief in 1916.

31

Number of colleges and universities where Beatrice Medicine taught

- As a child, she pretended to be a teacher. Her siblings were her students.
- She helped start the Wakpala Public School on the Standing Rock Reservation.
- Shortly before she died, Medicine received a special award from the Council on Anthropology and Education. The award was for lifelong dedication to education in anthropology.

CULTURAL ANTHROPOLOGY

Anthropology is the study of humans. Cultural anthropologists study how humans live and understand the world. They compare how different groups of people live. They try to understand changes within groups and why they happen.

2

Eugenie Clark: Shark Lady

Eugenie Clark was born in New York City in 1922. Her mother was Japanese and her father was American. She was two when her father died. When she was nine, she started spending Saturdays at the New York Aquarium. She wanted to know all about the fish there.

Clark earned college degrees in zoology. In 1950, she received her PhD from New York University. She learned to scuba dive so she could study sea creatures up close. She studied giant crabs, poisonous fish, and manta rays weighing 2,200 pounds (998 kg). Sharks were her favorite fish to study.

In 1958, Clark's work showed that sharks are intelligent. Before then, sharks were viewed as mindless eating machines. She discovered sharks in Mexico that do not need to swim to survive. She became known as "Shark Lady."

Clark started a marine laboratory in Florida in 1955. This would become the Mote Marine Laboratory. She made her last dive when she was 92. Clark died a year later, in 2015.

THE RED SEA

The Red Sea is between Africa and the Arabian Peninsula. It is home to coral reefs and more than 1,000 species of fish. Oceanic whitetip sharks catch their prey close to the water's surface. Clark began research there in the early 1950s. She made many discoveries. One was the Moses sole. This fish produces a natural shark repellant. Clark helped make the Red Sea an underwater sanctuary.

72

Number of submersible dives Eugenie Clark made in her lifetime

- A submersible is a vehicle that goes to the depths of a body of water.
- Without a submersible, divers can only go to around 200 feet (60 m) deep using scuba gear.
- One of Clark's deepest dives was 12,000 feet (3,658 m). She discovered whale sharks living at a depth of 3,200 feet (975 m).

3

Carol Shaw: Video Game Pioneer

Carol Shaw in 2017.

Carol Shaw was the first woman to design a video game for a major company. She was born in 1955 in Palo Alto, California. Her father taught mechanical engineering. She played with trains and cars instead of dolls. Math was her favorite subject in school.

In 1977, Shaw received a bachelor's degree in electrical engineering. She began working at Atari while finishing a master's degree in computer science. Atari was one of the first companies to make video games people could play at home.

Shaw designed her first Atari game in 1978. At that time, video game designers worked on every part of a game. They did much of their math by hand on paper. In 1980, *3D Tic-Tac-Toe* became the first of her games to be sold in stores. She was one of the best programmers at Atari. Other games she completed there were *Video Checkers* and *Super Breakout*.

In 1982, Shaw went to work for Activision. They released her game *River Raid* in 1983. This game featured a jet that blasted enemies as it flew down a river. It was a huge

THINK ABOUT IT

Today, only about 25 percent of workers in the gaming industry are women. Why is that number so low? Try to find out. What can be done to increase it?

15,000

Number of points needed to become an official River Raider

- Official River Raiders could mail pictures of their scores to the company. They would receive a *River Raiders* clothing patch in return.
- In the *River Raiders'* manual, Shaw invited gamers to send her a note with their thoughts on the game.
- The manual calls Shaw a Computer Science scholar.

success. Shaw was able to retire early because of that game.

Shaw was awarded the Industry Icon Award at the Game Awards in 2017.

Shaw won many awards for "Best Action Game."

4

Annie Easley: Human Computer

Annie Easley was an African American mathematician. She was also a rocket scientist and a computer programmer. Born in 1933 in Birmingham, Alabama, she was raised by a single mother. Easley loved school and was good at math. Her mother told her she could do anything if she worked hard enough.

Easley graduated high school at the top of her class. She studied pharmacy at Xavier University in New Orleans, Louisiana. After two years, she left school and got married. She and her husband moved to Cleveland, Ohio. There were no pharmacy schools in Cleveland. She had to find something else to do.

In 1955, Easley read an article about human computers. These were people who could do complex math in their heads. Two weeks later, she started working as a human computer at NACA. NACA stands for the National Advisory Committee for Aeronautics. It would later become NASA, the National Aeronautics and Space Administration.

While working full-time for NASA, Easley took classes at Cleveland State University. She earned her bachelor's degree in mathematics in 1977. She spent 34 years working at NASA. She faced racial and gender discrimination and was never

Annie Easley.

Easley at NASA in 1955.

100+

Number of unmanned launches that used the Centaur rocket

- Annie Easley worked on the Centaur. She went to Cape Canaveral, Florida, to watch some of the launches.
- The Centaur is known as America's workhorse in space. It is still in use today.
- It was involved in many historic flights, including the 1997 *Cassini* launch to Saturn.

promoted. She kept learning new things. When computers became more sophisticated, she learned how to code.

Easley worked on many important projects. One was an early battery technology. It was later used in hybrid vehicles. She fought discrimination by recruiting more women and people of color to work for NASA. She died in 2011 at age 78.

5 Beatrice "Tilly" Shilling: A War-Winning Invention

Without Beatrice "Tilly" Shilling, World War II might have had a different ending. She was born in 1909 in Hampshire, England, to a middle-class family. She bought a motorcycle at age 14. She learned to take it apart and put it back together. At 15, she decided to become an engineer.

Shilling left school at 17 to study under Margaret Partridge. Partridge owned an electrical engineering company and cofounded the Women's Engineering Society (WES). With her help, Shilling became one of the first women to attend the engineering program at the University of Manchester.

In 1932, Shilling got her bachelor's degree in electrical engineering. She received her master's degree in mechanical engineering a year later. She started racing motorcycles. In 1936, she began working for the Royal Aircraft Establishment (RAE).

At the beginning of World War II (1939–1945), the British *Spitfire* and

Beatrice "Tilly" Shilling.

A British *Spitfire.*

Hurricane fighter planes had serious technical issues. Unlike Germany's planes, these British fighter planes could not go upside down without causing the engine to shut down.

In 1940, Shilling invented a fix for this problem. It was called the RAE restrictor. It was easy to install. Many experts believe the British would have lost the war without it. Shilling worked for the RAE until 1969. She died in 1990.

106

Speed in miles per hour (171 km/hr) Shilling achieved on her motorcycle at the Brooklands motor track in England

- She was awarded the Brooklands Gold Star in 1934.
- Her motorcycle was a 500cc Norton International that she adjusted for maximum speed.
- She waited to marry her husband, George, until he earned his own Brooklands Gold Star. That happened in 1938.

6

Sonja Lyubomirsky: Happiness Researcher

Sonja Lyubomirksy has spent much of her life studying happiness. She is a psychologist. This is a scientist who studies the human mind—how it works and how it affects behavior. Lyubomirsky's research looks at how happiness changes over time and what people can do to increase their happiness.

Lyubomirksy was born in 1966 in Moscow, in what was then the Soviet Union. Her family emigrated to the United States when she was nine. They settled in the suburbs of Washington, DC. She learned English from American TV.

In 1989, Lyubomirsky earned her bachelor's degree in psychology from Harvard University. She did her graduate studies at Stanford in California. Her advisor encouraged her to study happiness. She finished her PhD at Stanford in 1994. She has been a psychology professor at University of California, Riverside, ever since.

Through her research, Lyubomirsky found that everyone has a "happiness set point." This is a person's normal level of happiness. When good or bad things happen, happiness may increase or decrease. But everyone will eventually go back to their happiness set point. Set points are determined in part by our genes. They are also determined by what we do and how we think. So it's possible to reset our happiness set point.

Sonja Lyubomirsky in 2016.

Factors Influencing Chronic Happiness Levels

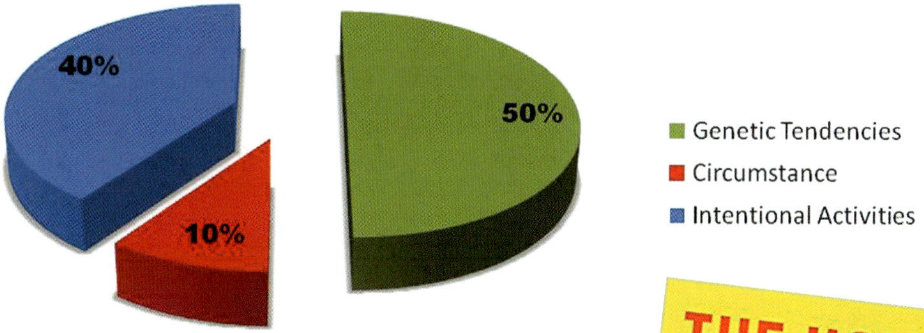

Adapted from Sonja Lyubomirsky's "Pursuing Happiness: The Architecture of Sustainable Change"

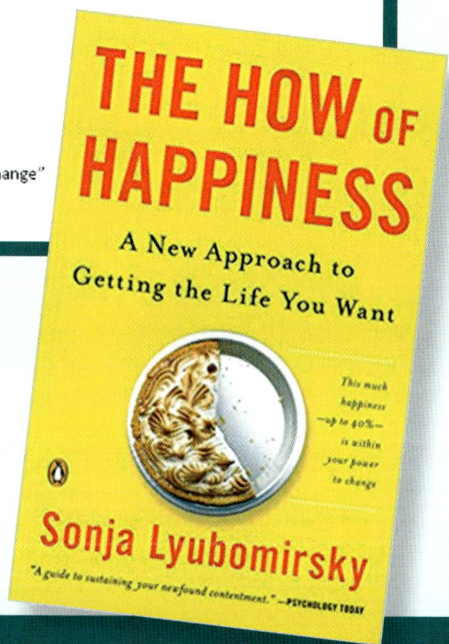

604

Number of hours it took Sonja Lyubomirsky to write *The How of Happiness*

- Published in 2007, this was the first book Lyubomirsky wrote for the layperson.
- It describes activities people can do to increase happiness. These include acts of kindness and giving thanks.
- Lyubomirsky's second book, *The Myths of Happiness*, came out in 2013.

THINK ABOUT IT

Lyubomirksy found that many people need to work hard to increase their happiness. What do you think that means? What might you do to improve your happiness, or the happiness of others?

7

Adriana Ocampo: A Leader in Space Exploration

As a child, Adriana Ocampo imagined traveling through space with her dog as her copilot. This passion for space exploration guided her to top positions at NASA.

Ocampo was born in 1955 in Columbia. She was raised in Buenos Aires, Argentina. At 14, she moved with her family to Pasadena, California. In high school, she started working at NASA's Jet Propulsion Laboratory (JPL).

4.1 billion

Number of miles (6.6 billion km) between Earth and Ultima Thule, the most distant object photographed in space

- The photos reached Earth on January 1, 2019. They were captured by the *New Horizons* spacecraft.
- Ocampo oversees the *New Horizons* team, which launched the craft in 2006.
- After the flyby of Ultima Thule, *New Horizons* kept going. It is learning more about the outer solar system.

In 1983, Ocampo earned her bachelor's degree in geology. She received her master's in planetary geology in 1999. She continued to work as a research scientist at JPL.

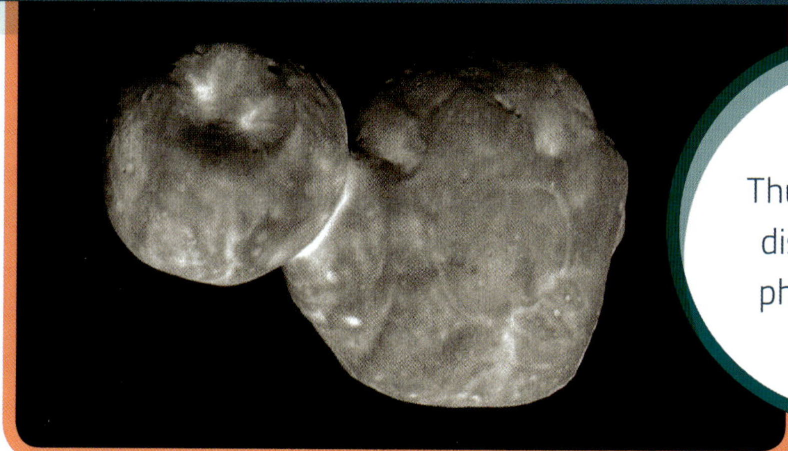

Ultima Thule, the most distant object photographed in space.

Her PhD in planetary geology is from VU University in the Netherlands.

Ocampo is best known for discovering the Chicxulub crater in Mexico. She has also mapped many planets. In 1984, she created the only photo atlas of Phobos, one of the moons of Mars.

Today, Ocampo is the head of NASA's New Frontiers program. This program is mapping Jupiter using a solar-powered craft. It is also working with the European Space Agency to study Venus.

THE CHICXULUB CRATER

In 1988, strange satellite images were presented at a conference. They showed a circle about 124 miles (200 km) across. Ocampo was in the audience. She knew it could be evidence of an asteroid. She studied the site on Mexico's Yucatán Peninsula. Her hunch was right. An asteroid hit that spot 66 million years ago. It killed over 70 percent of life on earth, including most of the dinosaurs.

8

Tiera Guinn Fletcher: Building a Rocket to Mars

Tiera Guinn Fletcher in 2017.

Tiera Guinn Fletcher was 21 when she became a rocket structural design and analysis engineer. She was born in 1995 in Mableton, Georgia. Her mother was an accountant. Her father was a construction worker.

When Guinn Fletcher was a little girl, she went grocery shopping with her family. Her mother asked her to add up the price of groceries as they shopped. She did this in her head and included the tax. From her father, she learned how math could be applied to building structures. At 11, she knew she wanted to be an aerospace engineer.

In 2013, Guinn Fletcher enrolled at the Massachusetts Institute of

322

Height in feet (98 m) of the SLS

- The SLS will be the world's most powerful rocket.
- In 2024, the SLS is scheduled to send astronauts to the moon's unexplored South Pole. The mission will include the first woman to go to the moon.
- It is scheduled to land humans on Mars in the 2030s.

WOMEN AND MINORITIES IN STEM

In 2016–2017, more than 60 percent of all STEM workers were white. Almost all STEM professions had more men than women. Fifty percent of women in STEM reported discrimination based on gender. Sixty-two percent of black STEM workers reported discrimination based on race. Meanwhile, studies have shown that diversity can make companies more profitable.

Technology (MIT). Starting in 2015, she spent her summers as an intern for the Boeing company. NASA had hired Boeing to work on the Space Launch System (SLS). Guinn Fletcher began working on the SLS in 2016.

Guinn Fletcher graduated from MIT in 2017. She still works for Boeing on the SLS. She's passionate about bringing more girls and people of color into STEM fields. STEM stands for Science, Technology, Engineering and Mathematics.

The SLS that Guinn Fletcher is working on for Boeing.

9

Barbara McClintock: Jumping Genes

She was born Eleanor McClintock in 1902 in Hartford, Connecticut. Her family moved to New York in 1908. When she wasn't reading, she was playing sports. Her parents changed her name to Barbara. They thought Eleanor was too feminine for their daughter.

1970

Year when Barbara McClintock received the National Medal of Science

- McClintock was the first woman honored with the medal.
- She received it from President Richard Nixon.
- During the award ceremony, the president told her he did not understand her work.

In 1919, McClintock started Cornell University. She earned both her bachelor's and master's degrees in botany. Botany is the study of plants. She received her doctorate in 1927.

McClintock studied corn, looking at its cellular and genetic makeup. She moved to any lab that would let her keep doing her research. In 1941,

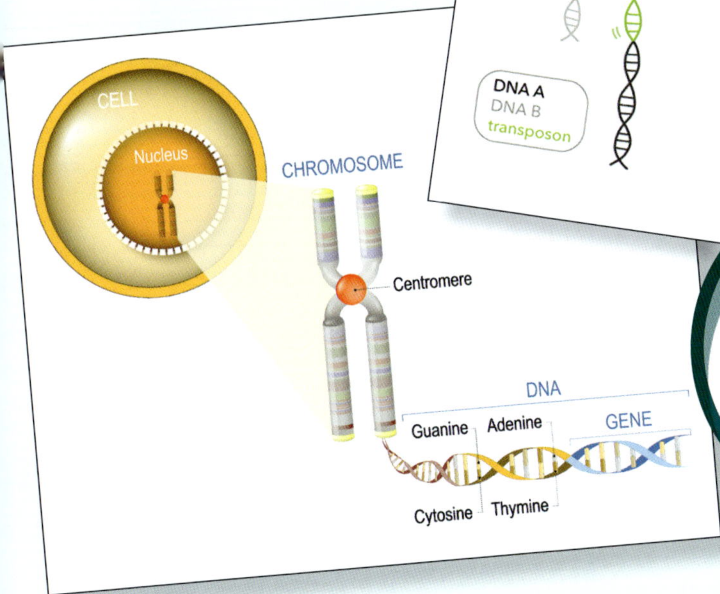

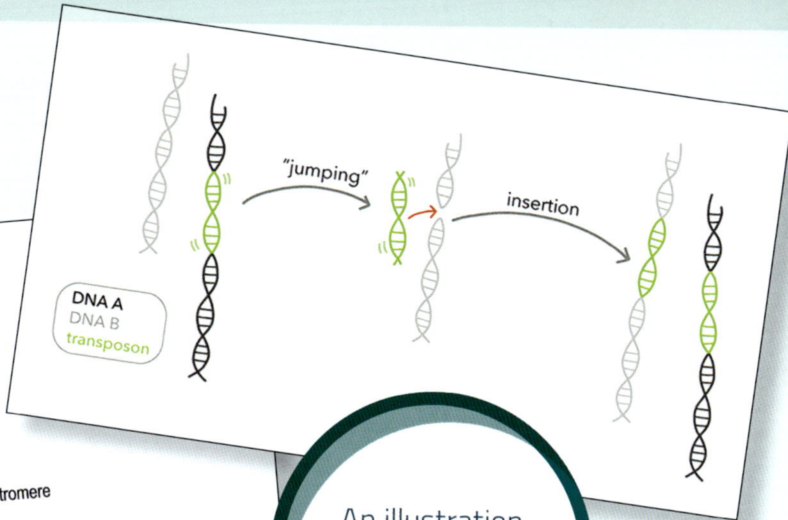

An illustration of DNA (left) and how it can jump.

she ended up at the Cold Spring Harbor Laboratory in New York. This is where she made some of her most important discoveries.

Every living thing is made of cells. Chromosomes live inside cells and carry DNA. DNA are instructions that tell cells how to form living things. These instructions are different for every organism. That's why every person is unique.

Some DNA can jump from chromosome to chromosome. These are called jumping genes. McClintock believed that when these genes jumped, they turned the DNA around them on or off. This was a groundbreaking idea. Scientists did not think DNA could change. McClintock began publishing her findings in the 1940s. In 1983, she won the Nobel Prize in Physiology or Medicine.

Scientists today know that jumping genes do not cause DNA to turn on or off. Still, McClintock's findings proved that DNA change. She died in 1992.

10

Angelica Lim: Teaching Robots to Feel

As a girl, Angelica Lim loved the robot maid Rosie from the TV cartoon show *The Jetsons*. She wondered if Rosie had human feelings. Lim has spent her career trying to create a real-life Rosie.

Angelica Lim in 2012.

She was born in California in 1985 and raised in Vancouver, Canada. Her mother was a computer programmer. Lim wanted to be like her mom. She received her bachelor's degree in computer science from Simon Fraser University in Vancouver.

In 2009, Lim went to Kyoto University in Japan. She earned her master's degree and her PhD in computer science. Her focus was on artificial intelligence (AI) and robotics. While studying for her PhD, she worked on Pepper. This was the world's first humanoid robot to go on sale to the public. The first 1,000 sold out in 60 seconds.

15

Number of languages Pepper speaks

- Over 2,000 companies around the world have purchased Pepper.
- In the United States, you can find Pepper at some HSBC banks and several Smithsonian Museums.
- Pepper is neither male nor female. But people usually call it a he or a she.

A conference attendee takes a selfie with Pepper.

DEVELOPMENTAL ROBOTICS

Developmental roboticists are caregivers to their robots. When a robot's battery is low, the roboticist treats it like a crying baby. Over time, the robot learns that having low energy is associated with sad human facial expressions and sad language, like "poor baby." When the robot's battery is charged, the roboticist plays with it. The robot learns that a sense of having high energy equals happy human facial expressions and language.

After graduating, Lim went to Paris to work for SoftBank, the company that created Pepper. Her job was to make Pepper act and speak like a human. Lim became a professor at Simon Fraser University in 2017. She works there today on developmental robotics. She named her lab the Rosie Lab.

11

Edith Clarke: Electrical Engineering Pioneer

Edith Clarke was born in 1883 in Ellicott City, Maryland. Both her parents died by the time she was 12. Her uncle sent her to a Maryland boarding school. She struggled with reading and spelling. But she did very well in mathematics.

At 18, Clarke went to Vassar College in New York to study math. She graduated in 1908. She began working as a human computer for AT&T in 1912. She solved complex math problems on paper or in her head.

38

Edith Clarke's age when she applied for a patent for her Clarke Calculator

- The calculator was used to solve complex calculations. These helped to find electrical current and power disruptions in power lines.
- It solved these equations 10 times faster than previous methods.
- It was the first invention in Smart Grid technology.

In 1919, Clarke became the first woman to earn a graduate degree in electrical engineering from the Massachusetts Institute of

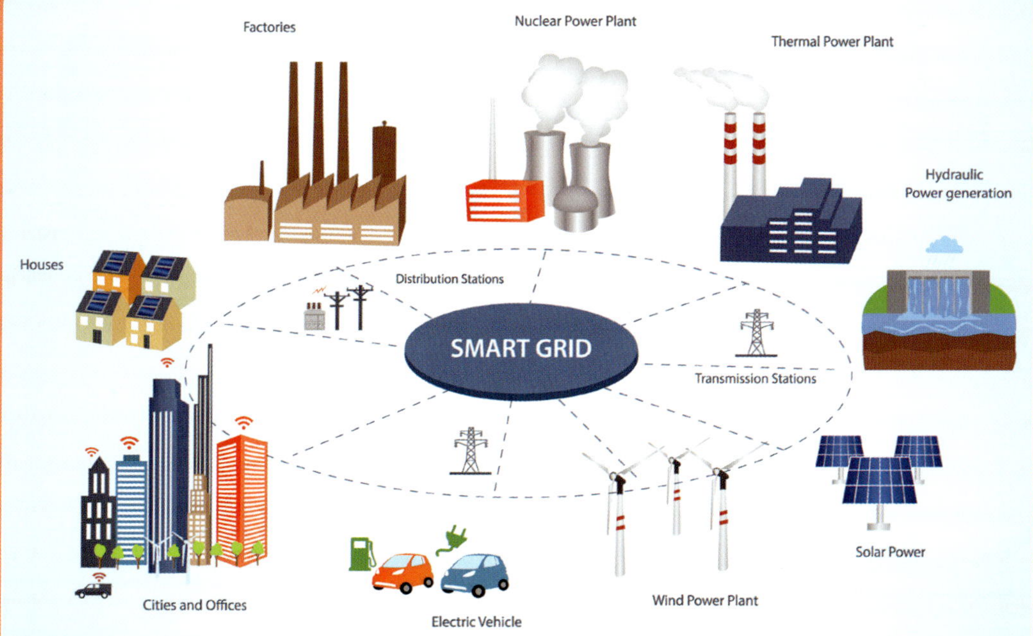

THE SMART GRID

The electric grid in the United States was built in the 1890s. It powers the nation's lights and electrical devices. This power comes from fuel, coal, nuclear reactors, dams, and renewable energy sources like wind and solar. Today, there are sensors that monitor how much power is used by a home or building. These sensors tell utility companies how much power is needed so it is not wasted. This back-and-forth communication is called the Smart Grid.

Technology (MIT). She took a job at General Electric (GE). In 1923, Clarke was given the title of electrical engineer. She was the first woman in the United States to have that title.

Clarke worked for GE for the next 25 years. In 1947, she began teaching electrical engineering at the University of Texas, Austin. She died in 1959.

12

Nina Tandon: Growing Bones

Nina Tandon in 2016.

All of Nina Tandon's siblings had vision problems. She turned to science to try to figure out why. Her early curiosity led to a career in biomedical engineering.

Tandon was born in 1980 in New York City. She was good at math and science. She received her bachelor's degree in electrical engineering from the Cooper Union in 2001. Her master's degree in bioelectrical engineering came from Massachusetts Institute of Technology (MIT) in 2006.

Tandon finished her education at Columbia University in 2012. She earned a PhD in biomedical engineering. Then she got a master's degree in business administration. When she was still a student, she created an electrical nose that could sniff out lung cancer.

In 2013, Tandon cofounded EpiBone. This company uses human stem

THINK ABOUT IT

Some people believe creating human cells in a lab is wrong. It raises questions about what it means to be human. Learn more about this. Then decide what you think.

3

Number of weeks it takes EpiBone to grow a bone

- So far, the company has successfully made bones for pigs.
- In May 2019, the Food and Drug Administration (FDA) said the company could start human trials. The first trial will be for patients with jawbone defects.
- EpiBone could go to market as early as 2023.

cells to grow bones. Stem cells can turn into many different types of cells in the human body.

EpiBone takes a three-dimensional X-ray of the area in a patient that needs a new bone. A 3-D printer creates a mold. The mold fits the area like a puzzle piece. Stem cells are taken from the patient. A machine called a bioreactor re-creates the environment inside a human body. The stem cells multiply in the bioreactor to fit the mold.

A bone that was grown in a mold by EpiBone.

Out of the Shadows

Caroline Herschel

The first professional astronomer, Herschel was born in Germany in 1750. Her brother, William Herschel, was also an astronomer. Together they created the first map of the Milky Way galaxy. Herschel lived much of her life in her brother's shadow. She made many important discoveries of her own, including finding eight comets.

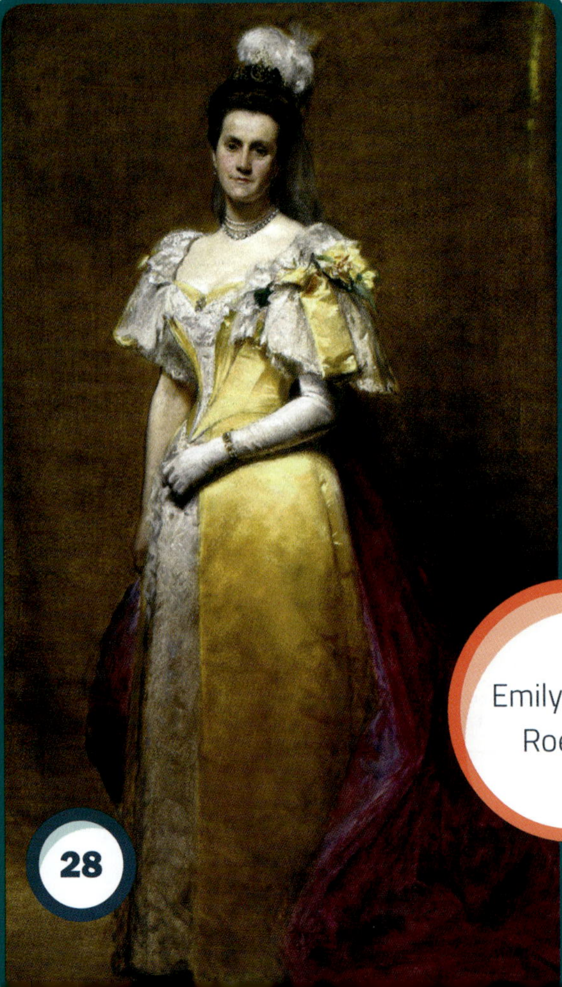

Emily Warren Roebling

She was born in New York in 1843. Her husband oversaw construction of the Brooklyn Bridge. In 1872, he became deathly ill. Roebling took over. She was engineer, messenger, and secretary. When the bridge opened in 1883, Roebling was the first person to walk across it

Emily Warren Roebling.

Frieda Robscheit-Robbins

Born in Germany in 1893, she moved to the United States as a child. She studied diseases with scientist George Whipple. Together they discovered a cure for anemia, an illness marked by a lack of red blood cells. Whipple was awarded a Nobel Prize for this in 1934. He did not acknowledge Robscheit-Robbins.

Mamie Phipps Clark

She was the first African American woman to receive a doctorate from Columbia University in 1943. Clark and her husband were psychologists. They proved that separating children by race damaged their minds and self-worth. This was important evidence in the 1954 *Brown v. Board of Education* case heard before the Supreme Court. This case ended segregation in schools.

Mamie Phipps Clark with her husband circa 1945.

Glossary

biomedical
Something that uses biology to create medicine.

engineer
A person educated in science and mathematics who designs and builds machines, products, or systems.

genetics
The study of how traits are passed down from parent to child.

geology
The study of rocks and soil to learn the history of a planet.

hybrid vehicles
Vehicles that use two or more sources of power.

indigenous
The original inhabitants of an area.

layperson
Someone without specialized knowledge in a field of study.

patent
A document that gives an inventor or company the right to be the only one to make or sell a product.

scuba
Equipment used to breath underwater. Stands for Self-Contained Underwater Breathing Apparatus.

social science
The study of human relationships.

sociology
The study of human interactions in society.

zoology
The study of animals and animal behavior.

Read More

Ignotofsky, Rachel. *Women in Science: 50 Fearless Pioneers Who Changed the World.* New York: Ten Speed Press, 2016.

O'Quinn, Amy M. *Marie Curie for Kids: Her Life and Scientific Discoveries, with 21 Activities and Experiments.* Chicago, IL: Chicago Review Press, 2017.

Saujani, Reshma. *Girls Who Code: Learn to Code and Change the World.* New York: Puffin Books, 2018.

Shetterley, Margot Lee. *Hidden Figures: The Untold True Story of Four African-American Women Who Helped Launch Our Nation into Space.* Young readers' edition. New York: Harper, 2016.

Stabler, David. *Kid Scientists: True Tales of Childhood from Science Superstars.* Philadelphia, PA: Quirk Books, 2018.

Index

About the Author

Brianna L. DeVore has a bachelor's degree in women's studies and works in the publishing industry. She lives in Minnesota with her husband, cat, and two dogs.